This journal is dedicated to
Those who run...

Our success depends on you!

Please take a moment to leave feedback on Amazon.com
And THANK YOU for your purchase!

Designed by Ruby Helton & M.L. Baldwin

PRODUCTIVE WEEK

- [x] ~~HW~~
- [x] ~~EMAIL MR. DAVE~~
- [ ] C·L·E·A·N ROOM
- [ ] PLAY GUITAR
- [ ] LEARN LAUNDRY
- [ ] COOK
- [ ] SHOP
- [x] ~~ART~~
- [ ] JOURNAL
- [ ] MEDITATE
- [x] ~~WORKOUT~~
- [ ] CALL AB
- [x] ~~PLAN DC TRIP~~
- [ ] PLAN CAMPING TRIP
- [x] ~~TEXT ELLA & SELINA & ASHA ABT FRIDAY~~
- [ ] REPAINT NAILS
- [ ] EAT HEALTHY
- [ ] BE GOOD
- [x] ~~LISTEN TO ALL THINGS GO~~
- [ ] COLLEGE APPS
- [ ] Y- CASE WORK
- [x] ~~SAT PREP~~

Don't be afraid to give up the good to go for the great

~ *Unknown*

A race is a
work of art
that people can
look at and be
affected in as
many ways
they're capable
of
understanding

~ Unknown

Few of us know
what we are
capable of
doing... we
have never
pushed
ourselves hard
enough to find
out.

~ *Alfred A. Montapert*

It's incredible
how many
emotions you
feel when
crossing the
finish line and
seeing that you
are No. 1.

~ Marcel Hirscher

You must expect great things from yourself before you can do them

~ Michael Jordan

I have always liked running, so it wasn't particularly difficult to make it a habit. All you need is a pair of running shoes and you can do it anywhere. It does not require anybody to do it with, and so I found the sport perfectly fits me as a person who tends to be independent and individualistic.

~ Haruki Murakami

Those who say it cannot be done should not interrupt those doing it.

~ Anonymous

The man who
can drive
himself further
once the effort
gets painful is
the man who
will win

~ Roger Bannister

You have to take a leap of faith to realize a dream, and this is something that a lot of people aren't willing to do.

~ Ron Bramlett

Experience has taught me how important it is to just keep going, focusing on running fast and relaxed. Eventually it passes and the flow returns. It's part of racing.

~ Frank Shorter

All it takes is all you got

~ Marc Davis

I believe you
make life what
you want it to
be; you can
reach goals
you never
thought you
could if you
keep at it.

~ *Mike Shine*

With self-discipline, all things are possible

~ Theodore Roosevelt

Out on the roads, there is fitness and self-discovery and the persons we are destined to be

~ *George Sheehan*

CC

The body does not want you to do this. As you run, it tells you to stop but the mind must be strong. You always go too far for your body. You must handle the pain with strategy... It is not age; it is not diet. It is the will to succeed.

~ Jacqueline Gareau

There will
come a point in
the race, when
you alone will
need to decide.
You will need
to make a
choice. Do you
really want it?
You will need
to decide

~ Rolf Arands

I think what endurance sports teach you is to stay dedicated, stay focused, and also to understand you're going to have ups and downs, but you need to keep running right through them.

~ *Kyrsten Sinema*

Champions do not become champions when they win the event, but in the hours, weeks, months and years they spend preparing for it. The victorious performance itself is merely the demonstration of their championship character

~ T. Allan Armstrong

The runner
must be a
fanatic for hard
work and
enthusiastic
enough to
enjoy the sport.

~ Anonymous

Success isn't given. It's earned. On the track, On the field, and in the gym. With blood, sweat, and the occassional tear.

~ Nike

**When the gun
fires you must
concentrate for
every second
on the way to
that finish line.
You should
know exactly
how long it will
take you to and
think about
every step of
the race you
are about to
run.**

~ Maurice Greene

I think sportsmanship is knowing that it is a game, that we are only as a good as our opponents, and whether you win or lose, to always give 100 percent.

~ Sue Wicks

It's not really about the competition. Your biggest challenge in a race is yourself. You're often racing against time. You're frequently running everything through your mind. You're always competing against preconceived ideas. It's not really the person next to you that you worry about.

~ Summer Sanders

Running is a mental sport and we're all insane.

~ Anonymous

Marathon running, like golf, is a game for players, not winners. That is why Callaway sells golf clubs and Nike sells running shoes. But running is unique in that the world's best racers are on the same course, at the same time, as amateurs, who have as much chance of winning as your average weekend warrior would scoring a touchdown in the NFL.

~ Hunter S. Thompson

I should just
stay composed
and run to the
finish line.

~ Asafa Powell

Failure will never overtake me if my determination to succeed is strong enough.

~ Og Mandino

Running leads to self-consciousness, self-awareness, and self-reliance.

~ Anonymous

You've done it before and you can do it now. See the positive possibilities. Redirect the substantial energy of your frustration and turn it into positive, effective, unstoppable determination.

~ Ralph Marston

Some people create with words, or with music, or with a brush and paints. I like to make something beautiful when I run. I like to make people stop and say, "I've never seen anyone run like that before." It's more then just a race, it's a style. It's doing something better then anyone else. It's being creative

~ Unknown

Shoot for the moon. Even if you miss it you will land among the stars

~ Les Brown

The task ahead
of you is never
greater than
the strength
within you

~ Unknown

If you set goals and go after them with all the determination you can muster, your gifts will take you places that will amaze you.

~ Les Brown

When you envision yourself doing something, you'll be surprised at how much that helps you to actually do it.

~ Selim Nurudeen

Eventually,
competition and
adventure wane, and
I enter my ibuprofen
phase. Tweaky
hamstrings and achy
knees restrict
mileage, but I
continue running
for health, sanity,
and the ritual of a
Sunday trail run
with like-minded
buddies. We discuss
the nagging injuries
that bedevil us, and
remember the good
old days when we
were kings.

~ Don Kardong

I've always
found that
anything worth
achieving will
always have
obstacles in the
way and you've
got to have
that drive and
determination
to overcome
those obstacles
on route to
whatever it is
that you want
to accomplish.

~ Chuck Norris

Desire is the key to motivation, but it's determination and commitment to an unrelenting pursuit of your goal - a commitment to excellence - that will enable you to attain the success you seek.

~ *Mario Andretti*

It's not how far
my feet will
run, it's how
far my mind
will take me

~ Anonymous

You must see yourself run the race over and over, time and time again. You must put yourself in critical positions and see how you would react in those positions before the race so when and if they do happen, the feedback is automatic.

~ Rodney Milburn

Running is the greatest metaphor for life, because you get out of it what you put into it

~ Oprah Winfrey

Gold medals aren't really made of gold. They're made of sweat, determination, and a hard-to-find alloy called guts.

~ Dan Gable

Racing teaches us to challenge ourselves. It teaches us to push beyond where we thought we could go. It helps us to find out what we are made of. This is what we do. This is what it's all about.

~ PattiSue Plumer

✦CC✦

Life's battles don't always go to the strongest or fastest man, But sooner or later the man who wins is the fellow who thinks he can

~ Unknown

Man imposes his own limitations, don't set any

~ Anthony Bailey

You can fight
without ever
winning, but
never ever,
win without a
fight

~ Unknown

Keep your dreams alive. Understand to achieve anything requires faith and belief in yourself, vision, hard work, determination, and dedication. Remember all things are possible for those who believe.

~ Gail Devers

cc

Running fills the cup that has to pour out for others. Running feeds the soul that has a responsibility to nourish. Running sets the anchor that limits the drift of the day. Running clears the mind that has a myriad of challenges to solve. Running tends to the self so that selfishness can subside.

~ Kristin Armstrong

Hard work beat talents when talent doesn't work hard

~ *Unknown*

To be number one, you have to train like you're number two

~ *Maurice Greene*

cc

You have to wonder at times what you're doing out there. Over the years, I've given myself a thousand reasons to keep running, but it always comes back to where it started. It comes down to self-satisfaction and a sense of achievement.

~ Steve Prefontaine

If speed kills,
I'm deadly

~ Anonymous